A GENTLE
INTRODUCTION TO
AGILE
SOFTWARE
DEVELOPMENT

STEPHEN HAUNTS

Table of Contents

This book is dedicated to my wife Amanda and my kids, Amy and Daniel, who are always putting up with my personal projects.

If you enjoy this book, then you might also like my other book called A Gentle Introduction to Lean Software Development, available on Amazon as a Kindle e-book or paperback.

ABOUT THE AUTHOR

Stephen Haunts has been a professional software and applications developer since 1996 and as a hobby since he was 10. Stephen has worked across many different industries including computer games, online banking, retail finance, healthcare & pharmaceuticals and insurance. Stephen started programming in BASIC on machines such as the Dragon 32, Vic 20 and the Amiga and moved onto C and C++ on the IBM PC. Stephen has been developing software in C# and the .NET framework since first being introduced to it in 2003.

As well as being an accomplished software developer, Stephen is also an experienced development leader and has led, mentored and coached teams to deliver many high-value, high-impact solutions in finance and healthcare.

Outside of Stephen's day job, he is also an experienced tech blogger who runs a popular blog called Coding in the Trenches at http://www.stephenhaunts.com/, and he is also a training course author for the popular online training company Pluralsight. Stephen also runs several open source projects including SafePad, Text Shredder, Block Encryptor, and Smoke Tester—the post-deployment testing tool.

INTRODUCTION

Who Is This Book For?

This book will appeal to many different audiences. If you are a developer, then this book will give you a good understanding of why Agile is beneficial to you, your team, and your employer. This might be the first agile project that you've worked on, and you want to understand why you're using Agile over Waterfall. This book will also be an excellent refresher on why you're using Agile if you're already on an agile project.

If you're a project manager, then this book will help you understand the difference between an agile project and the more traditional Waterfall project. As teams become more self-directed when working on a project, a project manager is still crucial to help ensure the teams are operating correctly and that the team delivers on time and budget.

If you're an IT or business leader and your company is considering adopting Agile, this book will also help you understand how this will work and what the benefits are to your organization. This book is split down into six main areas.

- Waterfall development and its problems,

- What is agile all about?

- Typical Agile misconceptions,

- Advantages and Disadvantages

- Extreme Programming (XP)

- Scrum

Waterfall Development and it's Problems

History of the Waterfall Model

The Waterfall development methodology was introduced by the computer scientist Winston Royce in 1970. Winston Royce first discussed the ideas of Waterfall software development in an article called <u>Managing the Development of Large Software Systems</u>. Winston Royce didn't refer directly to the model in his paper as Waterfall development. This article was about a process that was flawed for software development. Royce's original design actually allowed for more repetition between stages of the model which Waterfall doesn't let you do.

Winston Royce's actual model was more iterative in how it worked and allowed more room to maneuver between stages. We will discuss a more frequentative way of working when we discuss Agile later on in this book. Although Royce didn't refer to this model as the Waterfall mode directly, he is credited with the first description of what we refer to as the waterfall model.

Royce's original article consists of the following stages, which we'll go into more detail on in a moment. Those stages are the

- Requirements Specification stage
- Detail Design stage
- Construction phase
- Integration
- Testing and Debugging
- Installation
- Maintenance

How Does Waterfall Work?

In Waterfall, the process is divided into separate stages, where the outcome of one stage is the input of the next stage. The first stage in a Waterfall will start with the Requirements covering all requirements analysis, where all of the requirements for the system being developed are recorded in a specification document. This requirements specification will then need to be signed off by another project stakeholder, usually from the business.

It is the responsibility of the business analyst on the project to create the requirements document, but if you are working on a smaller team, then it could be done as a collaboration between team members. In this stage of the waterfall cycle, the business analyst, or persons writing the document try to capture all the requirements and features of the system from the key business stakeholders. This could include the complete set of functionality, any business rules that need automating, and any other operational processes from a company and regulatory perspective.

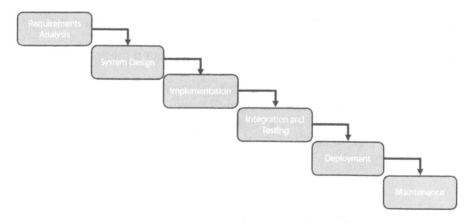

Figure 1 The waterfall software development process

The next stage is System Design. The Requirement specifications from the first stage are inspected, and the system design is put together. This design helps in specifying the design requirements, and also helps with creating the overall systems architecture. In this stage, it is the technical members of the team, which includes developers and architects that decide how the overall system will be built.

Once the system design phase is complete, we move into the implementation phase. This is where the developers on the team take the previous software design and start writing the code to make it work.

After the implementation phase, we then move into the integration and testing phase. This is where a testing team will bring all the system components together and test them as a single product. The test team at this stage should have a detailed testing plan that they work towards by either performing manual testing or developing automated tests. Once the testing team has completed its work and signed off the system as fit and proper, it is then ready for deployment to the end users who can start seeing the benefits.

Once the solution has been deployed into production, it will then go into a maintenance phase. During this period, if the end users report any defects, they will get fixed, tested and then redeployed into production.

If any of these fixes end up being very large in scope, then the decision might be made to start the waterfall again by redefining the requirements, designing, implementing, testing and deploying. If this happens though, it can be quite time-consuming, which wouldn't lend itself to fixes that have to be made in urgency.

Where Is Waterfall Suitable?

While in the agile world, there is a lot of emphasis on saying that waterfall is not suitable, there are some software projects where the Waterfall methodology is appropriate. Let's take a look at a few.

First, Waterfall is suitable if your software projects requirements are already well defined and documented, but how often is that the case though? From my own experiences as a software designer and developer, I can't remember any of the many projects I've delivered where the requirements have been clear from the start so that they can be captured in a document that doesn't change as the project rolls on.

Next, the product definition must be stable. Again, I can't think of a single project where this has been the case, as external factors like a change in the marketplace or a shift in business priorities mean that your product will evolve. I have worked on many projects where the final delivered product was entirely different from what was initially specified. Under Waterfall, this shouldn't happen, but in reality, what you are building can change. There is nothing wrong with this, but it does fight against software delivery process.

Next, the technology should be well understood. This means that developers should understand the technologies that they're going to be using and how they work. Once you enter the implementation and construction phase of the project, developers usually have to work toward very rigid and set timescales. In my experience working on a Waterfall project, a lot of effort is expelled on the requirements and design phases, which normally eat into the time needed actually to develop the code.

Next, Waterfall works best on projects that are short, and by short, I mean projects that are around 2-4 months in total. The longer a project runs for, the more chance there is that the requirements and product definition are becoming out of date.

Finally, Waterfall works best when all of your product team are available to work together. It is quite normal for a development team to have a pool of resources that might be shared out between many different projects. If another project is over-run for any reason, you may not have all your people available at the time when they are required. This can significantly impact a project's timescale and put delivery dates at risk.

Advantages and Disadvantages of Waterfall

In a moment, we'll take a look at some pros and cons of the Waterfall model. But before we do, I first want to cover some of the main high-level advantages and disadvantages to this development process.

The first advantage is that by splitting your project deliveries into different stages, it is easier for an organization to maintain control over the development process. This makes it much easier for schedules to be planned out in advance. This makes a project manager's life much more comfortable. It's for this reason I've found that experienced project managers tend to favor the Waterfall process as it can make their lives much easier. By splitting a project down into the various phases of the Waterfall process, you can easily departmentalize the delivery of your project, meaning that you can assign different roles to various departments and give them a clear list of deliverables and timescales. If any of these departments can't deliver on time for various reasons, it is easier for a project manager to adjust their overall plan.

Unfortunately, in reality, I've seen the method adapted where the implementation phase gets squeezed more and more, which means the development team has less time to deliver a working solution, and this can mean quality suffers and shortcuts tend to be taken. It's usually code-base unit and integration testing that gets affected first. This has a knock effect that the testing teams in the test phase get a solution that contains more problems, which makes their lives very hard. So, while departmentalization is seen as an advantage, it can quickly become a disadvantage if another team is late delivering their part of the project.

Now let's take a look at some of the high-level disadvantages. The Waterfall model doesn't allow any time for reflection or revision to a design. Once the requirements are signed off, they're not supposed to change. This should mean that the development team has a fixed design that they're going to work towards. In reality, this does not happen, and changes in requirements can often result in chaos as the design documents need updating and re-signing off by stakeholders.

By the time the development team starts their work, they are pretty much expected to get it right the first time, and they're not allowed much time to pause for flaws and reflection on the code that they have implemented. By the time you get to the point where you think a change of technical direction is required, it is usually too late to do anything about it unless you want to affect the delivery dates. This can be quite de-motivating for a development team, as they have to proceed with technical implementations that are full of compromises and technical debts. Once a product has entered the testing stage, change is virtually impossible, whether that is to the overall design or the actual implementation.

Now we've seen some of the high-level advantages and disadvantages. Let's take a more in-depth look at more of the benefits of the Waterfall model. The waterfall is a simple process to understand, and on paper, it seems like a good idea for running a project. The waterfall is also easier to manage for a project manager as everything is delivered in stages that can be scheduled and planned. Phases are completed one at a time where the output from one phase is fed into the input of the next stage. Waterfall works well for smaller projects where the risk of changing requirements and scope is lower. Each step in Waterfall is very clearly defined. This makes it easier to assign clear roles to teams and departments who have to feed into the project. Because each stage is well defined, it makes a milestone set up by the project manager easier to understand. If you're working on a stage like Requirements Analysis, you should know what you need to deliver to the next phase, and by when.

Under Waterfall, the process and results of each stage are well documented. Each stage has clear deliverables that are documented and signed off by key project stakeholders. The Waterfall model fits very neatly into a Gant chart, so a project manager is happier when they can plan everything out and view a project timeline in an application like Microsoft Project.

The biggest disadvantage of the Waterfall model is you don't get any working software until late in the process. This means that your end users don't get to see their vision come to life until it is too late to change anything. It can be tough for non-technical people to be clear about how they want an application to operate, and it isn't normally until they can visualize an application that they can give good feedback. You can mitigate this a bit by doing some prototyping in the system design phase to help users visualize their system, but there is nothing like giving them the actual working code to try out.

The Waterfall model can introduce a high level of risk and uncertainty for anything but a small project. Just because a set of requirements and design has been signed off, does not mean that the conditions won't change. The Waterfall is all about getting the requirements, design, and implementation right the first time, which is a grand idea in a perfect world, but in the real world it is very rarely the case, and this is a big risk to a project. The more complexity that is involved increases the risk of the change needed further down the line. Complexity in the system is also very hard to implement and test, and can often cause delays in the later stages of the Waterfall software development lifecycle.

If you're working on a project where change is expected, then Waterfall is not the right model for you. I've worked on projects for a financial services company, where variations in financial law were causing compliance regulations to change. Unfortunately, these rules are very open to interpretation, which meant the legal team was involved at a very early stage. This meant that the interpretation changed a few times during the project. If this had been a Waterfall project, we would have been in big trouble, as projects frequently come with a sturdy and fixed set of deadlines.

This was a perfect fit for an agile project. If you are working on a large project and the scope changes, the impact of this can be so expensive and costly, that the original business benefit for the project can evaporate and then the project is canceled. I've seen this happen a couple of times, and it's a real shame, as projects that show real promise are stopped due to restrictions in the process.

Finally, the integration and delivery of a project are done as a "Big Bang" on a Waterfall project. This means you're introducing massive amounts of change all at once. This can quickly overwhelm testing teams and your operational teams.

History of the V-Model

Now that we've finished taking a look at the traditional Waterfall model let's take a look at a model that builds on Waterfall. This is called the V-Model. As opposed to the Waterfall method, the V-Model was not designed to run in a linear fashion. Instead, the process is turned upwards after the implementation or coding stage is complete which makes the V shape. The V-Model is based on the idea of having a testing stage for each development stage. This means that for every single stage in the development cycle there is a directly associated testing phase. This is a strict model, and the next step starts only after the completion of the previous stage. Now let's take a look at how the V-Model works.

How Does the V-Model Work

With the V-Model, the detailed testing of the development stage is planned in parallel, so there are verification steps on one side of the V and the validation stages on the other side. The coding and implementation phases join both sides of a V-Model together.

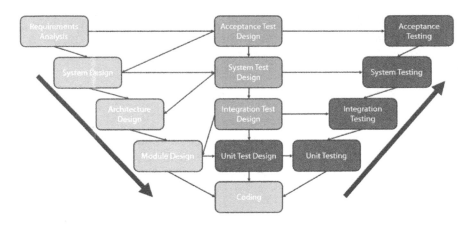

Figure 2 The V-Model software development process

When you draw out the V-Model, it can look a bit complicated, but once you break it down, it's quite straightforward. First is the Requirements Analysis phase. This is the first phase of the product development process where the customer requirements are understood which requires collaboration with the client to understand his/her expectations. As most clients are not entirely sure about what they need, the Acceptance Test Design planning is completed at this stage as any business requirements can be used as input for the acceptance testing.

Next is System Design. Once you understand the requirements, you put together a complete design of the entire system. This design will include both software and hardware/infrastructure design. At the same time as preparing the system design, you would usually put the system test design together too so that your test teams can pre-plan their testing activities.

Then we have the Architectural Design. The architectural design will look at a much broader design focus than the system design. This may even result in multiple designs being proposed that balance vendors, costs, and other factors.

Unit-tests are a critical piece of any development process and help identify bugs in the code early so that the team has early visibility of any breakages caused by other dependencies. Once all of these design phases are completed, you can then proceed to the coding stage. The language used in the coding stage along with the architecture should already have been agreed upon by this point, allowing developers to make an immediate start.

Next, we enter the validation phase of the V-Model. First, we have unit testing. Unit tests designed in the Module Design stage are run against the code during its validation stage. Unit testing is a test at the code level and helps eliminate bugs at an early stage, although all defects cannot be uncovered by unit testing alone, they do give a good indication quickly as to any breakages that may or may not occur. This does mean that the developers have to be quite disciplined in writing good unit tests that add value and don't just check language features. Following on we have the Integration Testing phase. Integration tests are performed to check the co-existing of different modules or components within the system; here we are making sure that all integration between various components within the system as a whole is working as expected.

After integration testing, we have system testing. System tests check the entire systems functionality and the communication between all other external systems. If you have integrated with 3rd party payment providers, for example, they will be tested at this stage. Most of the compatibility issues you are likely to face will be uncovered during system test execution.

The final phase is Acceptance Testing. Acceptance Testing is associated with the Business Requirements Analysis phase and involves testing the products in a user's environment by the users. Acceptance tests uncover the compatibility issues with other systems available in the user environments. Acceptance testing also discovers a non-functional issue such as load and performance defects in the user environments.

Where Is the V-Model Suitable?

The V-Model is similar to Waterfall as both models follow a defined path through their stages. To make the V-Model as successful as possible, you will need to make sure your project requirements are well-defined, documented, and thought out so that they don't change over time. You also need to be sure that a product definition is stable. This is much easier to describe than put into practice, project changes over time due to a change in the company's priorities or market conditions are the main reason for problems here. The technology being used must be well understood before you get to the coding phase, there's often no margin for your developers to learn on the job, due to the need to deliver to tight timescales.

Once you leave the Requirements Analysis and Definition phases, you cannot have any ambiguous requirements, because like waterfall there is simply no margin for changing them later without causing a lot of disruption.

Finally, as with Waterfall, the V-Model is ideally suited to shorter project timescales. The longer the project runs, the more risk is introduced of the requirements changing over time.

Advantages and Disadvantages of the V-Model

The V-Model shares very similar advantages and disadvantages of the more traditional Waterfall model, but it is worth covering them again, as it helps set the scene for our discussion about agile software development. The first advantage is that the V-Model is quite easy to understand and apply. It fits well with companies that have different departments all feeding into the development process. The V-Model is also easy to manage, as you only proceed to the next phase of the model once the current phase is complete. This makes it easier for project managers who manage the project. Again, as with Waterfall, the V-Model is not flexible to changes in requirements. This means you'll have to repeat the phases in the models to make sure all your documentation is intact. A shift of needs can be quite disruptive to a project, so you need to ensure the requirements are right from the start.

In reality, what often happens is that if there are any changes to the requirements, to reduce the cost of disruption, the process is just bypassed to get the changes through quicker. If you're going to circumvent a process, there's no point in having the process in the first place?

The V-Model works best on small projects where the risk of changing requirements is less than that of a larger project. The V-Model is easy to understand, and the actual validation phases are suitable for mature test departments. Project managers tend to like the V-Model as it is easier to manage against the plan. The rigidity of the model maps well to a project manager's view of the world and makes their job a bit easier.

The V-Model can introduce a high level of risk and uncertainty for anything but a small project. Just because a set of requirements in design has been signed off, does not mean the conditions cannot change. The V-Model is all about getting the requirements, design, and implementation right the first time, which is a grand ideal, but in the real world this is an infrequent case, and this is a significant risk to a project. I talked about how the V-Model is better for small projects, but it is possible to have a small but very complex project. The more complexity that is involved increases the risk of change being needed further down the line. Complexity in a system is also very hard to implement and test and can often cause delays in the later stages of the V-Model software development lifecycle.

If you're working on a project where change is expected, then a V-Model is not the right model for you. Once you're starting to test your solution, going back to make changes in the code, other than to fix defects, can be very challenging and expensive. The biggest disadvantage of V-Model is that you don't get any working software until late in the process. This means that your end users don't get to see their vision come to life until it is too late to change anything. It can be tough for non-technical people to be clear about what they want an application to do, and it isn't normally until they can visualize the application that they can give excellent feedback.

Agile Software Development

What Is Agile?

Agile software development is a set of software development practices that promote an evolutionary design with teams that can self-organize themselves. Agile software development inspires evolutionary development, adaptive planning methods and early delivery of value from your software to your end customers.

The word agile was first linked to the development of software back in 2001 when the Agile Manifesto was devised by a group of visionary leaders and software developers.

Unlike traditional development practices like the waterfall, agile methodologies such as Scrum and Extreme Programming are focused around self-organizing, cross-discipline teams who practice continuous planning and implementation to deliver value to their customers.

The primary goal of agile software development is to deliver working software that gives value sooner to the end user. Each of these methods emphasizes ongoing association between technology and the business for whom you are developing the software. Agile software methodologies are considered lightweight in that they strive to impose a minimum process and overhead within the development lifecycle.

Agile methods are adaptive which means support changes in requirements and business priorities throughout the whole software construction process. Changes in requirements are to be embraced and welcomed. With an agile software development project, there is also a considerable emphasis on empowering teams with collaborative decision-making. In the previous chapter, I talked about how the Waterfall-based development process follows a set series of stages which results in a "big bang" deployment of software at the end of the process.

One of the main ideas behind Agile software development is that instead of delivering a "big bang" release into production at the end of the project, you release multiple versions of working code to your stakeholders continually. This will allow you to prioritize features that will deliver the most value to the users sooner so that your organization can get an early return on their investment, and that investment comes in the form of money spent and time consumed in development and planning. The number of deliveries into production that you do depends on how long and complicated a project is, but ideally, you would deliver working software at the end of each sprint or iteration.

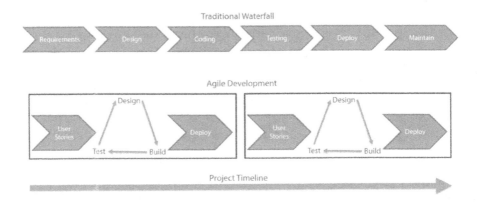

Figure 3 Agile vs Waterfall

Another good way to visualize the premise of Agile is the above diagram. What this diagram shows is that with Agile you deliver incrementally instead of all at once. You should hold this thought in your mind as we progress through the rest of the book.

A Brief History of Agile

There have been lots of attempts to improve software development methodologies over the years, and many of these have looked at working iteratively, these new practices didn't go far enough when trying to deal with changing requirements of customers.

In the 1990's, a group of industry software thought leaders met at a ski resort in Utah to seek and define a better way of developing software. The term "agile software development" emerged from this gathering. The term was first used in this manner and published in the now-famous Agile Manifesto. The agile manifesto was designed to promote the ideas of delivering regular business value to your customers and made it necessary that you should focus on a collaborative, cross-functional team to make this happen.

The Agile Manifesto 4 Core Values

The Agile Manifesto is split into 4 core values.

1. Individuals and interactions over processes and tools
2. Working software over comprehensive documentation
3. Customer collaboration over contract negotiation
4. Responding to change over following a plan

For the first of the core values, we have "Individuals and interactions over processes and tools." People build software systems, and to do this properly, they all need to work together and have good communication between all parties. This isn't just software developers but includes QA, business analysts, project managers, business sponsors, and senior leadership, and anyone else involved in the project at your organization. Processes and tools are necessary but are irrelevant if the people working on the project can't communicate and work together efficiently.

For the second of the core values, we have, "Working software over comprehensive documentation." Let's face it, who reads a 100-page product spec? I certainly don't. Your business users would much prefer to have small pieces of functionality that are delivered quickly so they can then provide feedback. These pieces of functionality may even be enough to deploy to production to gain benefit from them early. Not all documentation is bad though. When my teams work on a project, they use Visio or similar tools to produce diagrams, and this is not an exhaustive list, employment environments, database schemas, software layers, and use-case diagrams. We typically print these out on an A3 printer and put them up on the wall, so they are visible to everyone. Small, useful pieces of documentation like this are invaluable. 100-page product specs are not. Nine times out of ten large items of documentation are invalid and out of date before you even finish writing them. Remember, the primary goal is to develop software that gives the business benefit, not extensive documentation.

For the third of the core values, we have, "Customer collaboration over contract negotiation." All the software that you develop should be written with your customer's involvement. To be successful in software development, you need to work with them daily. This means inviting them to your stand-ups, demoing to them regularly, and inviting them to any design meetings. Only the customer can tell you what they want. They may not be able to give you all the technical details, but that is what your team is there for, to collaborate with them, understand their requirements, and to deliver on them.

For the fourth and final of the core values, we have, "Responding to change over following a plan." Your customer or business sponsor may change their minds about what is being built. This may be because you've given them new ideas from the software you delivered in a previous iteration. It may be because the company's priorities have changed or new regulatory changes come into force. The key thing here is, you should embrace it. Yes, some code might get thrown away and some time may be lost, but if you're working in short iterations, then this time lost is minimized. Change is a reality of software development, a reality that your software process must reflect. There's nothing wrong with having a project plan. In fact, I'd be worried about any project that didn't have one; however, a project plan must be flexible enough to be changed.

Agile Methodology Overview

Which agile project methodologies are commonly in use today?

First of all, we have Scrum. Scrum is a lightweight project management framework that is based on an interactive working model. Ken Schwaber, Mike Beedle, Jeff Sutherland, and others, contributed to the development of Scrum over many years. Over the last few years, Scrum has earned growing popularity in the software development community because of its simplicity, proven success, and improved productivity, and its ability work to with various other engineering practices promoted by other Agile methodologies, such as Extreme Programming.

Next, we have Extreme Programming or XP as it is also known. Extreme Programming was initially devised by Kent Beck and has emerged as one of the more popular and controversial Agile methods. Extreme Programming is a disciplined approach to delivering high-quality software faster and consistently. It emphasizes lots of customer engagement, rapid feedback loops, continuous testing, continuous planning, and teamwork to deliver working software at a frequent release cadence, typically every 1-3 weeks. Whereas Scrum is a project management framework, XP is much more of an engineering discipline. It is very common for teams to adopt Scrum yet borrow different engineering practices from XP.

The original XP recipe is based on four simple values:

1. Simplicity
2. Communication
3. Feedback
4. Courage

There's also 12 supporting practices. These are:

1. Planning game
2. Small releases
3. Customer acceptance tests
4. Simple design
5. Pair programming
6. Test-driven development
7. Refactoring
8. Continuous integration
9. Collective code ownership
10. Coding standards
11. Metaphors
12. Sustainable pace

Next, we have the Crystal methodology. The Crystal Method is a lightweight, adaptable approach to software development. Crystal is comprised of a family of methods like Crystal Clear, Crystal Yellow, and Crystal Orange, whose unique characteristics are driven by factors, like team size, system criticality, and project priorities. The Crystal family looks at the fact that each software project may require a different set of policies, processes, and practices to meet the project's requirements.

Next, we have the Dynamic Systems Development Method, or DSDM as it is most commonly known. DSDM dates back to 1994 and evolved to provide an industry standard project framework for what was commonly called rapid application development or RAD for short.

While RAD was famous in the early 1990's, the RAD approach was quite unstructured and as a result of this DSDM was formulated to add structure to the idea of rapid application development. Since 1994, DSDM has evolved to provide a comprehensive foundation for managing, planning, executing, and scaling agile and iterative software development projects. DSDM is based on nine key principles that revolve around business need and value, active user involvement, empowered teams, frequent delivery, integration testing, and business stakeholder collaboration.

Then we have Feature-Driven Design or FDD for short. Jeff De Luca originally developed the feature-driven design. FDD is a model-driven, short-iteration process. It begins with establishing an overall model shape; then it continues with a series of 2-week, design-by-feature, built-by-feature iterations. The features are small and useful in the eyes of the client. FDD designs the rest of the development process around feature delivery using the following eight practices:

1. Domain object modeling
2. Developing by feature
3. Components and class ownership
4. Feature teams
5. Inspections
6. Configuration management
7. Regular builds
8. Visibility of progress
9. Results

Next, we have Lean software development. Lean software development is an iterative method initially developed by Mary and Tom Poppendieck. Lean software development owes its heritage to the Lean enterprise movement of companies like Toyota. Lean software development focuses heavily on the team to deliver value to the customer and on the efficiency of the value stream and the mechanisms that provide that value.

The main principles of Lean include:

• Eliminating waste
• Amplifying learning

- Deciding as late as possible
- Delivering as fast as possible
- Empowering the team
- Building in integrity
- Seeing the whole

Lean eliminates waste by focusing on only parts of a system that deliver real value to businesses. Lean Software Development puts emphasis on the speed and efficiency of development and relies on rapid feedback between programmers and customers.

Roles within an Agile Team

Agile teams, while part of a department or company, are primarily focused on their software development goals. Each team should also be focused on their team's overall vision. This means a team should be very reactive in doing whatever is required to get the job done. This means that team members may have to do work that is outside their usual skill set. This should be embraced and encouraged. A cross-functional and adaptive team is much more likely to succeed.

Most teams will, of course, have some standard areas of expertise and specialisms and you may also have people with the particular domain or product knowledge, but there should be flexibility in team players expected roles and responsibilities. It should also be common for team members to have access to the business as a whole and this shouldn't just be limited to a select few. You should have people who are tasked with making sure the team follows the development process and someone who co-ordinates requirements gathering with the business, this would typically be referred to like the product owner if you are working within the Scrum framework.

Teams will normally have some form of a leadership role within the team. In Scrum, this person is the Scrum master. On Agile teams, this person aims to enable and ensure the success of the team. This type of leader is frequently referred to as a servant leader. This role is entirely different to the direct transactional leader on a Waterfall project.

One goal of an agile team should be to improve as a team every day. The larger the organization, the more complicated group structures can get. Cross-project teams, shared services, operations, configuration management, and database administration can all come into play, but the goal remains the same, define a software project and cross-functional team capable of delivering on that plan and empower the team to do so.

Common Agile Misconceptions

Agile Misconceptions

When a team is new to agile, it can be hard for them to adjust to a new way of working, especially if they're used to working under a Waterfall-based methodology. When a team is faced with changing how they work, it is common for excuses to be made by team members as they resist the change. Not all teams are like this, but in my experience, it is quite common to hear many different misconceptions, in this chapter we'll discuss many of these mistakes and why they come about.

Agile is ad-hoc, with no process control: To be agile, you need to adhere to the Agile Manifesto, but following the manifesto doesn't mean you are using a defined process. The manifesto describes a set of ideas. There are various processes and project management templates that you can apply to your projects to help them become agile. Extreme Programming and Scrum are the two most popular, but Lean and Kanban are also becoming very popular.

When you try to implement the manifesto items, you generally need to apply lots of common sense and pragmatism to help you get to your goal, but if you want to warp a more formal process around the "how" of agile, as opposed to the "why", then you would need to apply something like Scrum or Extreme Programming, which gives you more formal processes like stories, iterations, stand-ups, demos, retrospectives, test-driven development, and pair programming.

Agile is wasteful without upfront planning: This assumes that your customer knows the details of all their requirements in advance. If this is true, then by all means, undertake comprehensive upfront planning. However, in reality, this is rare and usually, leads to greater waste of having taken design and development work that was ultimately unnecessary.

Agile development is not predictable: When working with an established agile team, you can bring a level of predictability to your development life-cycle and business as you will be regularly delivering working software to your customers. The frequency of these releases will be set with your stakeholders, but in the ideal situation, you should have releasable code at the end of each sprint.

Agile is faster and cheaper: Running an Agile team doesn't mean you will finish a project quicker or for less money. It isn't a direct money saver in that respect. What being agile is about is delivering value to the business sooner. You head toward working versions of the software quicker. At the end of each development iteration, you're supposed to have working software to demo to the business. You may not have all their requirements in place, but what is there will work. This means re-thinking about how you plan your workload in each iteration. Instead of delivering horizontal slices, for example, the data access layers this iteration and user interface in the next iteration, you think in vertical segments.

This means you deliver defined pieces of functionality in an iteration that may encompass work on the user interface and data access layer. It's a mind shift change that I've seen teams struggle with if they are used to working horizontally, but when they finally get it, the efficiency of a team is increased remarkably. Being agile is also about being able to respond to change. Requirements can vary, and business can change partway through delivery. I've worked with teams who treat this is a real negative thing. If you want to be agile, you need to expect and embrace that things will change. The tools and processes of Scrum, for example, are designed to help you react to these changes in a more efficient manner.

Agile teams don't write documents or do planning: Practising agile on your team is not an excuse to avoid planning or documentation writing. Agile is an act of doing what is needed at the time of requiring it, and encourages continuous planning and documentation, but only when it is necessary for specific customer requirements. This allows teams along with their customers to decide if the plan or document adds value to the product. Depending on what type of company you work for, formal documentation may not be something that you can avoid. For example, if you work in a very densely regulated environment, then there's lots of upfront documentation that may be needed for evidence and submission to a regulatory body. If this is the case, then the delivery team will need to take this documentation into account.

I prefer to work with large diagrams instead of large documents of text. If you can, get these diagrams printed out onto A3 paper, and then put them up all over the walls, so you have something to refer to in your standups. With the planning side of this, you still need to do it. At the beginning of each iteration or sprint, you should have a planning session where you allocate user stories for iteration. The number of stories you allocate will be based on the estimates given and the velocity of the previous iteration.

Agile means no commitments: It can be a common belief that people on agile teams do not want to make promises and that you have a team of developers churning away until someone shouts "We're Done!" A successful agile team should be very transparent about what they intend to deliver to their users. When using methodologies like Scrum and Extreme Programming you have a concept of a backlog which contains all your high-level user stories and tasks for a given sprint or iteration. As you define the workload for a sprint, this should be seen as a guide to what the team intends to deliver. Once a sprint or iteration is setup, it will not change, but it may be required that you have to change your plan part way through a sprint. This could result in a partial re-plan in that sprint/iteration, or wait until the next sprint. XP doesn't like changing a sprint once it is in flight, and this is more acceptable under Scrum, but no law says you can not alter the commitment if required. What is important is that a level of trust is built up between the team and the business stakeholders.

An agile project will never end: This might be true in some situations. You should continue to work on a project while the customer continues to get business value. Most products in any industry have a point of diminishing returns. This is the ideal time for an agile project to end. This decision should come from the business though, for it is them that you are delivering value to. Agile works for projects, teams, and organizations of any size, not just small projects. This doesn't mean it'll necessarily work for all teams, but size is rarely a factor. Large and complex projects and organizations are often excellent candidates for an agile transformation, where it is difficult or impossible to know all of your customer's requirements in advance.

Agile is the solution to all your problems: Agile is a change in approach and culture that comes with its own set of benefits and issues. If you're working in a well-established team that has not been following any agile processes, then changing them over will not be an instant transformation. You need to do it slowly, make sure everyone has a say in decision-making. If you don't, you may get resistance from team members who fear change, which is a perfectly normal human characteristic. Convincing your team isn't the biggest hurdle though, your biggest challenge is making sure that your leadership team understands and wants to adopt Agile as a way of working. Once you have achieved this and had leadership buy-in, then the rest of the adoption just takes time and patience as everyone adjusts.

There's only one way to do agile: The original Agile Manifesto consists of four core values and 12 principles. It doesn't document any actual implementation details. There are many interpretations of Agile that form different methodologies, like Scrum, Extreme Programming, Kanban, and Feature-Driven Development, to name a few. Each style has its benefits and weaknesses, and you must evaluate your situations to decide which methodology is the best fit for your team. Extreme Programming and Scrum are the two most popular methods in use today, but also Lean, and Kanban are becoming very popular. As long as you stick to the Agile Manifesto's values and principles and deliver high-value software regularly to your customers, you should be considered agile.

Agile development doesn't require upfront design: It is a common misconception that agile teams just make it up as they go along. This isn't true, what is more, realistic is that agile teams should make sure design happens at the last responsible point in time. For coding activities, it is more acceptable that the code is designed as the developer works on it, and refactors to a better design as they go along, this is what evolutionary design is all about. More system-wide and architectural design can be scheduled in 1 or more sprints/iterations ahead of time. By only designing as you need to, you can react to changes in requirements more efficiently. When you try to design the entire system up front, any design decisions that you make are likely to be redundant by the time you come to implement them.

Advantages and Disadvantages

Advantages of Agile

As you've seen in the past chapters, agile software development is an entirely different approach to software development compared to the more traditional Waterfall development model. Let's take a look at some of the advantages to using Agile as an approach.

Customer satisfaction by rapid, continuous delivery of useful software: Your clients and users will be satisfied because you are continually delivering value to them with usable software. This is a stark contrast compared to that of the traditional Waterfall product delivery process. Now if your customers are used to Waterfall, they may find it strange adjusting to having working software sooner. The big downside of Waterfall is that you deliver large pieces of functionality towards the end of the project life-cycle. This means all throughout the development stages of Waterfall your project is incurring the cost with no return on investment. By delivering working pieces of functionality sooner and more regularly, you're giving your users an opportunity to get a return on their investment sooner. Sure, they may not have all the functionality they need up front, but they can start to make use of the solution to make their lives easier and start realizing the benefits sooner. People and interactions are emphasized rather than process and tools.

Agile is focused very heavily on people and the interactions between people rather than the processes and tools: This is a core value of the Agile Manifesto. The reason this is important is that it is the input from your team and customers that will ultimately make your project a success, as opposed to what tools you use. Continual collaboration throughout the entire development cycle of your project enables everyone involved to build up a good working relationship that will be based on trust. This trust-based working relationship is crucial when building software incrementally.

Continuous attention to high-quality code: When working with Agile, you're working short iterations and only build what is necessary to satisfy the requirements for that iteration and nothing else. This forces you to keep your design simple, which is essential as simplicity helps you develop testable, and therefore, more reliable systems. Developers understand and choose many solutions to solve a businesses problem, and these are choices that reflect a craft that balances design, use, and support. Developers provide the technical assistance to the team that enables them always to keep code quality high. Developers like to use the latest techniques for keeping their implementations straightforward and clean without having to rework any of their solutions.

Some of these techniques include refactoring. Refactoring is the process of improving the design of existing code without changing its behavior. To make changes to the structure of the code, refactoring uses a quick succession of small, well-defined steps that can be verified as safe or functionally equivalent. Refactoring is most often done in conjunction with test-driven development where unit tests and simple design make it easier to refactor safely.

Simple design: Keeping your design simple, and not repeating code, helps you keep a level of maintainability for your system. If you design your code to be modular, then you can reduce coupling between objects, which leads to an overall, more robust system.

Test-driven development: Test-driven development is a way of improving the design of your code by writing unit tests, which expresses what you intend the code to do, making that test pass, and continually refactoring to keep the design as simple as possible. TDD can be applied at multiple levels, for example, unit tests and integration tests. Test-driven development follows a rigorous cycle. You start by writing a failing test. Then you implement the most straightforward solution that will make that test to pass. Then you search for duplication in the code and remove it. This is often called Red-Green-Refactor and has become almost a mantra for many test-driven design practitioners. Understanding and even internalizing this cycle is key to being able to use test-driven design to solve your problems.

Embracing changes in requirements: Your clients or business partners may want to change their mind about the software that is being built. This might be because you have inspired them with new ideas from the software you delivered in a previous iteration. It could be because the company's priorities have changed. The key thing here is that you should embrace the change. Yes, some code may get thrown away and some time is lost, but if you're working in short iterations, then this lost time is minimized. Change can be terrifying at first for clients and partners alike, but when both sides are prepared to leap, it can be mutually rewarding. In some ways, Agile is a simple idea, but the reality is that it can mean different things to different people, especially depending on their role in the software development process. One of the key things, though, is to be open to change, not just to move in traditional ways of organizing projects but to adapt your use of Agile itself.

Early return on investments: Another advantage to releasing features early is you get a return on your investment sooner. Running a software development team is expensive. You have permanent developers and testers, as well as consultants with expensive day rates. There's also business analysts, project managers, as well as other hardware and software costs. These are all costs to the business. By releasing early and generating revenue from your product, you can start to offset some of the initial investment and development costs. On the flip side of that, if you have a more Waterfall-based approach where you end up with a "big bang" deployment after a year or so, you will have already spent significant amounts of money to fund the development with nothing to show until at the end.

Feedback from your customers: If you release early, this means you can start to solicit feedback from your clients a lot sooner. These customers could be public-facing customers or business sponsors. I've worked on many projects where the business customer specifies requirements, which you then build, only for the customer to want changes once they have something they can use. This always seems to happen. It's tough for someone to specify a system without having something to play with. You can use prototyping software to help, but there is nothing like giving them actual functionality early on to start using. One of the principles of Agile is to embrace change in the requirements. This should be expected, so giving your customer something they can feedback on sooner will allow them an opportunity to make changes sooner without causing much disruption.

Feedback from real customers: Once you start getting feedback from real customers, you can start incorporating changes and new ideas from the feedback into the product. It is much more cost effective to make changes early on in a product's development cycle than it is to wait until the end once a large release has been achieved. It's not just customer feedback that helps you build the right product, by testing your product early in the marketplace, you can gauge customer uptake and see how popular the product will be, and continually deliver better quality.

Everything we have discussed so far has business benefits or culminates in the fact that you should be providing a better-quality product with every release. By releasing earlier and soliciting feedback, you can learn from the product performance earlier, and use this information to create something of higher quality. Product and system development are all about continuous learning and improvement, which is much easier to do when you're delivering a project by being agile. It doesn't matter whether you're using Extreme Programming, Scrum, DSDM, Crystal, or any of the other project management frameworks. If you stick to the core values in the Agile Manifesto and routinely deliver high-value functionality early to your customers, monitor their usage and listen to their feedback, you can apply this learning to the ongoing development and increase quality as you go along.

Disadvantages of Agile

Now that we have taken a look at some of the advantages let's now take a look at some disadvantages.

Hard to assess the effort required at the beginning of the software development life cycle: One complaint I have often heard from business leaders and project managers alike, is that compared to Waterfall, it is hard to quantify the total effort and cost to deliver a project. On the one hand, I can see why they would think this, especially when they come from a regimented Waterfall process world. Indeed, it is harder to quantify how long the total project will take entirely, but the mitigation for this is that a product will be delivered incrementally by giving the users the most valuable requirements first, meaning you can plan for the coming sprint and maybe a few sprints ahead to provide a specified amount of functionality.

It can be very demanding on a users' time: Active user participation and collaboration with the users of your system are required throughout the development cycle with Agile. This can be very rewarding and ensures you deliver the right product to your users. It's an essential principle with Agile to make sure that a user's expectations are well-managed, and the definition of failure is not meeting your user's expectations. However, this level of participation can be very demanding on the user and require a big commitment for the duration of the project. I have been in this situation many times where the business users love the idea of what Agile can bring to them, but they don't like the extra amount of time they have to spend on the project as they have to still fit this in with their current workloads.

Costs can increase as testers are required all the time instead of at the end of a project: Testing is an essential part of an agile project during sprints or iterations. This helps to ensure quality throughout the project without the need for a lengthy and unpredictable test phase at the end of a project. However, this does mean that testers are needed throughout the entire product development lifecycle, and this can dramatically increase the cost of resources on your team. This extra upfront cost does save you money in the long run though as you are continually having people test your code. Having a combination of manual testing and automation testing is the best way to drive up the quality of your product. The cost of a long and unpredictable test stage at the end of a waterfall project can, in my experience cause the enormous unexpected losses when the project overruns and they frequently do overrun.

What Are Your Department's Biggest Challenges?

Let's now take a look at whether Agile is right for your team, and if you are prepared for moving to a more agile way of working. If you are working at a new company or on a brand-new team, starting out with Agile can be very easy, but if you're working in a larger, well-established organization that has been using more of a Waterfall-based approach, the switch to Agile can be challenging to do.

Let's start off by looking at possible challenges faced by your department.

Is your department under pressure to achieve hard deadlines? Are there too few people to get the work done, or insufficient budget allocations? Are staff not as productive as they could or should be? Are the business processes, equipment or communication channels that they use slowing them down? Is there too much corporate knowledge in the heads of a handful of employees, or are low-quality outputs creating the need for constant fire-fighting and damage control? Every IT team can benefit from using agile approaches, but the teams that have the most significant issues also have the most to gain from agile approaches that specifically target these issues. This is why agile methods are ideally suited to teams where there are ongoing problems with the quality of delivered solutions, providing software solutions within agreed timelines and budgets, delivered solutions not adequately supporting business requirements, or high staff turnover rates or low staff productivity levels.

The amount of benefit your team will get from implementing Agile is also linked to some risks.

- The likely hood for requirements changing while the product is being developed, and this includes changes in user needs, staff departures, business priority shifts, and funding.

- External changes where there are variations in the market demand, announcements from competitors, and the availability of new technologies

- The sustainability of your current overheads, including development costs, implementation costs, maintenance, and support.

If your products are based on predictable and replicable business processes with a minimum likelihood of changing requirements, then your team will not achieve the same level of benefit from Agile as one that is more susceptible to solution requirements that are likely to evolve. The same goes for teams where the current software solutions are delivered on time, align well with the business requirements, and require minimal ongoing support to address quality and usability issues. In each of these situations, Agile methodologies can provide some degree of benefit to the team, but not the dramatic benefit that the teams with more dynamic and less sustainable software solutions can achieve. Ultimately, the more your team is faced with changing requirements, and unsustainable IT overheads, the better positioned you are to receive returns on your Agile investments.

Are You Prepared for Agile?

For some organizations, notably larger and older ones, the answer to the question, are your people prepared for change, is likely to be no.

The idea of implementing methodologies that encourage the evolution of business requirements instead of relying on upfront documentation, empowering the project team to self-organize instead of controlling their daily activities, and replacing reams of documentation with face-to-face communication may seem a bit daunting for some staff. That is particularly the case for those that have grown comfortable with their normal day to day routines and just live with the problems in their code and the solution they are developing. A great debilitation when trying agile is people saying, "This is the way we have always done it." These types of individuals are usually very resistant to change.

If your staff is hesitant at first, you may find that giving agile a try on a donor project in your team will help get them familiar with and motivated by agile. If after trying one or two agile projects your staff is still uncomfortable working directly with the business areas, supporting changing requirements as the project progresses, and self-managing their work, it may be that agile approaches are just not suited to your organization's working culture.

If on the other hand, your team reacts well to the trial projects then this paves the way for you more fully adopting these methodologies. Going agile does require a change in attitude for managers and leadership too. Traditionally it might have been more common to have direct control over what your team members are working on, but with agile you need to take a different approach.

Management style needs to be more like servant leadership where managers are there to remove any barriers from the teams' progress and encourage the team to think for themselves and organize their workload. After all, developers are paid very well, so you need to have a more realistic level of trust that they will do the right thing.

Another interesting thing about the dynamic of self-organizing teams is that as they progress, they improve ongoing motivation for employees. Project team members know that their continued ability to self-manage their work depends on their regular delivery of higher-value business outcomes. Additionally, because they are the ones who identify what work can and cannot be achieved in each iteration, they are motivated by their responsibility to reach these outcomes. This combination of factors is heightened by the satisfaction and pride that staff members feel when they produce tangible outputs that truly meet the needs of the organization.

Extreme Programming (XP)

Now that we have looked at some theory of agile software development, it's time now to take a look at some agile methodologies.

In this chapter, we'll look at Extreme Programming or XP for short. As we look at Extreme Programming, we'll first look at its history; then we'll look at an overview of the methodology, following that we'll look at the typical Extreme Programming activities, values, principles, and practices. Finally, we'll finish up by looking at the different rules of Extreme Programming, which are split down into five categories, planning, managing, designing, coding, and testing.

History of Extreme Programming

Extreme Programming is a methodology in Software Development which promotes improving software quality and being able to respond to changing customer requirements. As an agile methodology, it supports more frequent releases to your end users and shorter development cycles. Other elements of Extreme Programming include programming in pairs or doing extensive code reviews, unit testing all of the code and avoiding programming of features until they are needed.

The name Extreme Programming comes from the idea that software engineering practices are taken to extreme levels within your team. For example, code reviews are a good practice, and under intense programming, they are taken to an absolute level by promoting continuous code reviewing by pair programming.

Kent Beck was the creator of Extreme Programming during his employment at the then-struggling Chrysler Comprehensive Compensation System payroll project or C3 as it was known in 1996. The project was designed to aggregate many different payroll systems into a single application.

Initially, Chrysler attempted to implement a solution, but it failed because of the complexity surrounding the rules and integration. From this point of crisis, Kent Beck and his team took over, effectively starting the project from scratch. The classic Waterfall development approach had been tried and failed, so something drastic was required. In Kent Beck's own words regarding Extreme Programming, he just made the whole thing up in two weeks with a marker in his hand and a whiteboard. Fundamentally, the C3 team focused on the business value the customer wanted and discarded anything that did not work towards that goal. Developers created extreme Programming for developers.

The XP team at Chrysler were able to deliver their first working system within one year. In 1997, the first 10,000 employees were paid from the new C3 system. Development continued over the next year with new functionality being added through smaller releases. Eventually, the project was cancelled because the prime contractor changed, and the focus of Chrysler shifted away from C3. When the dust settled, the 8-member development team had built a system with 2,000 classes and 30,000 methods. XP had been refined and tested and was now ready for the wider development community.

Overview of Extreme Programming

Extreme Programming can be described as a software development discipline that organizes people to produce high-quality software more productively. Extreme Programming attempts to reduce the cost of changing requirements by having multiple short development cycles rather than one long cycle as is seen in Waterfall.

With Extreme Programming, changes are a natural, inescapable, and desirable aspect of software development projects. You should plan and expect changes in requirements, instead of thinking you will get a complete and stable set of requirements upfront that will not change. Extreme Programming also introduces four activities such as coding, testing, listening, and designing. There are also five values, such as communication, simplicity, feedback, courage, and respect, four principles, such as feedback, assuming simplicity, and embracing change.

There are also 12 practices that are split into four groups. These groups are fine-scale feedback, continuous process, shared understanding, and programmer welfare. And finally, there are 29 rules divided into the following five groups. These groups are planning, managing, designing, coding, and testing. We will cover all these activities, practices and rules in the remainder of the chapter.

Activities

Extreme Programming describes four primary activities that are performed within the software development process. These activities are

- Coding
- Testing
- Listening
- Designing

Coding

Coding is an essential product of the Extreme Programming process. Without code, there is no working product. To a programmer, a well written and structured system serves as good documentation to his or her fellow programmers. This coding can involve many different languages such as C#, Java, Python, C, C++, F#, JavaScript, and much more.

Testing

With Extreme Programming, the developer will practice what is called test-driven development. This is where you write a failing test first and implement just enough code to pass the test, and then refactor the code to a better structure, while tests still pass. The programmer will strive to cover as much of their code in unit tests as they can to give them a good level of overall code coverage. This code coverage will help build up the trust that the system operates as expected.

You cannot be sure of having a working system or product unless you have tested it. With Extreme Programming, you ideally want to automate as much of your testing as possible so that you can repeat the testing frequently. This can be done by writing unit tests. Unit tests will test a small block of code in isolation of any external dependencies like databases or the file system.

Listening

The next activity to discuss is that of listening. Programmers must listen to what the customers need the system to do and what business logic is required. The requirements from the customer are documented as a series of user stories.

These user stories help to drive out a series of acceptance tests, which help determine when a user story is completed and working as expected. Once user stories and acceptance tests are written, the developers can then start their planning and estimating.

Designing

The final activity is designing. To create a working system or product, requirement gathering, coding, and testing should be all you need, but in reality, software systems are very complicated, so you'll often need to perform a level of overall system design that you may not have expected. This doesn't mean that you'd to create a several-hundred-page design document, as that could be quite wasteful, but there is definite value in producing an overall system design where you look at the whole structure of the system and its dependencies.

Ideally, you want to create a system where all of the components are as decoupled from each other as they can be so that a change in one part doesn't require sweeping changes across the rest of the system.

Values

There are five core values that Extreme Programming is based on. Although Extreme Programming defines many rules, which we'll look at in a bit, Extreme Programming is more wired to work in harmony with your personal and corporate values. The five values are:

- Communication
- Simplicity
- Feedback
- Respect
- Courage

Communication

For any project to succeed you need to have good communication between the development team and all the stakeholders. By having good communication on the team, it makes it a lot easier for the team to respond to changes in requirements from the end users.

The customer sees the team's progress every day and can adjust the work schedule as needed, as the client collaborates with the developers to produce tests to verify that a feature is present and works as expected.

When you have a question about a feature, you should ask the customer directly. A 5-minute face-to-face conversation, peppered with body language, gestures, and whiteboard drawings, communicates more than an email exchange or conference call can, so removing the communication barriers between customers and developers increases your flexibility.

Clear communication about goals, status, and priorities not only allows you to succeed but makes everything else in the project run smoothly too.

Simplicity

Simplicity means building only the parts of the system that need to be built. It means solving today's problems today and tomorrow's problems tomorrow. Predicting the future is very hard, so building in excessive complexity early on is very costly. Once you're armed with communication and feedback, it's much easier to know what you need. If you practice simplicity, it should be as easy to add a feature when it becomes necessary.

Feedback

Feedback means asking questions and learning from the answers. The only way to know what a customer wants is to ask them. The only way to know if the code does what it should do is to test it. The sooner you can get feedback, the more time you have to react to it. XP provides rapid, frequent feedback. Every XP practice is part of building a feedback loop. The best way to reduce the cost of change is to listen to and learn from all of those sources as often as possible. This is why XP concentrates on frequent planning, design, testing, and communicating. Rapid feedback reduces the investment of time and resources in ideas with little payoff.

Failures are found as soon as possible, within days or weeks rather than months or years, and this feedback helps you to refine your schedule and your plans even further than your original estimates may have ever allowed you to. It will enable you to steer your project back on track as soon as someone notices a problem and identifies when a feature is finished, and very importantly where it will cost more or less than previously believed. It builds confidence that the system does just what the customer wants.

Courage

Making hard decisions can be tough and it takes a lot of courage. If a feature isn't working, fix it. If some code is not up to standard, improve it. If you're not going to deliver everything you promised on schedule, be up front and tell the customer as soon as possible. Courage is a difficult virtue of applying. No one wants to be wrong or to break a promise. The only way to recover from a mistake, though, is to admit it and fix it.

Delivering software is challenging, but meeting that challenge instead of avoiding it, leads to better software.

Respect

Respect within your team underlies the other values previously mentioned. Intrinsic rewards like motivation, enjoyment, and job satisfaction beat extrinsic rewards like employee-of-the-month awards or physical rewards every time. Everyone should contribute value to the team, even if it's simply enthusiasm. Developers should always respect the expertise of the customers and vice-versa, and managers should always respect the developer's right to accept responsibility and receive authority over their work.

Principles

Frequent and prompt feedback is very useful with Extreme Programming as it reduces the cycle time from feedback to action being taken to resolve any feedback. Rapid action on feedback is critical to a team learning through frequent contact with their customers. This also means the customer has a clear insight into the system that is being developed and can give feedback and steer development as needed.

Unit tests contribute significantly to the rapid feedback principle. When writing code, running the unit tests provides direct feedback as to how the system reacts to any changes made to it. If a developer's code changes mean there is a failure in some other part of the system, the automated unit test suites will show the failure immediately, alerting the developer of the incompatibility of his change within other regions of the system, and the necessity of removing or modifying his change.

With software development methodologies like Waterfall, the absence of automated unit tests means that such a code change, thought to be harmless by the developer, would have been left in place, appearing only during integration testing, or even worse showing up once the product has been put into production. Identifying which code changes created the problem, can be a difficult task, and not one you want to perform very often.

Extreme Programming rejects these ideas. Extreme Programming applies small incremental changes to the codebase over time. For example, a system might have small releases every three weeks. When many little steps are made, projects customers and sponsors will have more control over the overall development process and the product being created.

For instance, if at one of the iteration planning meetings it appears the customer's requirements have changed dramatically, programmers can embrace this and plan new requirements for the next iteration. Under waterfall development, changes in requirements are seen as a hazardous and costly thing to happen. Even small changes can have a very large impact on a program of work. If any of the main fundamental requirements change under Waterfall, it could put the entire project at risk of being cancelled. This risk is drastically minimized under an agile development framework like Extreme Programming.

Practices

In Extreme Programming, 12 practices are followed. These are split into four main groups that aim to define software development best practices. These are:

1. Fine-scale feedback
2. Continuous process
3. Shared understanding
4. Programmer welfare

Fine-scaled Feedback

First up are the practices for fine-scale feedback. First of all, there's pair programming. Pair programming means that all code is produced by two people programming on one task at one workstation. One programmer is writing the code at the keyboard, while the other developer is thinking about the problem being solved and looking at the big picture. This programmer is also reviewing the code that the other developer is writing.

Programmers trade roles after short periods of time. The pairs are not fixed. Developers switch partners frequently so that everyone has good coverage over the whole codebase. This way, pair programming can also enhance team-wide communication.

The planning game is the primary planning process for Extreme Programming. The game is a meeting that occurs once per iteration, typically once a week or every two weeks. The planning game is broken into two parts. First, there is release planning. This is focused on determining what requirements are included in which near-term releases, and when they should be delivered. The customers and the developers are both parts of this meeting.

Release planning consists of three phases. The first is the exploration phase where the customer will provide a list of requirements for the product. These will be documented on what are called story cards. Then there's the commitment phase. Within this phase, the customer and developers will commit to what functionality will be delivered and in what time frame.

Then there's the steering phase. In this period, the plan can be adjusted, new requirements can be added, and conditions can be changed or removed. After release planning, we have iteration planning where the tasks for the developers are defined. In this process, the customer is not involved. The primary purpose of the planning game is to help guide the product into delivery. Instead of predicting the exact dates when deliverables will be needed and produced, which is difficult to do, the aim is to steer the project to completion.

Then we have test-driven development. Unit tests are code-based tests that exercise the functionality of the system being developed. Within Extreme Programming, unit tests are defined before the code is written. This helps the programmer think through the possible failure scenarios for the system that needs to be implemented.

First, developers write a minimal test that should break because the functionality hasn't been fully implemented yet. Then the developers verify that the code does indeed fail the test. Then they will write the minimum amount of code to make the test pass. Then the unit tests are run to make sure that they pass. You should then modify or restructure the code to a better design while the tests still pass.

Within XP, the customer is the one who uses the system being developed. Extreme Programming says that the customer should be on hand at all times and available for questions. For instance, a team developing a healthcare dispensing system should include a pharmacy business partner to answer questions and assist with the design.

Continuous Process

Now let's take a look at the practices for a continuous process. First, we have continuous integration. The development team always needs to be working on the latest version of the software by using a source code repository like TFS or Git.

The source code repository should ideally run an automated build against the code as it is checked in and then run the automated unit tests. This will test the integrity of the code being submitted to the repository. Continuous integration of the source code in the repository will avoid delays later on in the product life-cycle caused by integration problems.

Next, we have refactoring or design improvements. XP advocates programming only what is needed today, and implementing it as simply as possible. Another symptom is that changes in one part of the code affect lots of other parts, Extreme Programming states that when this happens, the codebase is informing you to refactor your code by changing the design which makes it simpler and more generic.

The delivery of the software is done by frequent releases of functionality creating value for the end user. Small releases help the customer to gain confidence in the progress of the project over time. Once you're building quality software, the whole team as a unit can feel good about the accomplishments they've achieved.

Shared Understanding

Coding standards are an agreed upon set of rules that the entire development team agrees to adhere to throughout the project. The standards specify a consistent style and format for source code within a chosen programming language, as well as various programming constructs and patterns that should be avoided to reduce the probability of defects.

The coding standards may be a set of conventions specified by the language vendor or custom-defined by the development team. These days, it's common to use a coding productivity tool such as ReSharper, CodeRush, or JustCode to help enforce these standards. These tools will be set up with a pre-defined set of rules, and as the developer is writing code, these tools will highlight violations of the coding standards, and in most cases, offer suggestions for fixes. They are excellent for ensuring consistency within a code base.

Next, we have collective code ownership, which means that everyone on the team is responsible for all of the code. This, in turn, means that everybody is allowed to change any part of the code. Pair programming contributes to this practice by working different pairs. All the programmers get to see all of the parts of the code.

A significant advantage of collective code ownership is that it speeds up the development process because when any errors are detected, then any developer can go in and fix them. By giving every programmer the right to modify the code, there is a higher risk of defects being introduced by developers who think they know what they're doing but do not foresee certain dependencies. Sufficiently well-defined unit tests help to address this problem. If unforeseen dependencies create errors, then when the unit tests are run they will show up as failures.

Next up we have, simple design. A keep it simple mentality should be approached when designing a system. Whenever a new piece of code is developed, the programmers should ask themselves, is there a simpler way to create the same functionality. If the answer is yes, then the more straightforward approach should be adopted.

Finally, with a shared understanding, we have the system metaphor. The system metaphor is a story that everyone, customers, programmers, and managers, can tell about how the system works. It's a naming concept for classes and methods that should make it easier for a team member to guess the functionality of a particular class or method from its name only. For example, a pharmacy healthcare system may create a dispensable drugs class for a dispensing system, and if the drug goes out of stock, then the system will return a warning when a check stock availability method is called on the dispensing drug's class. For each class or operation, the functionality is obvious to the entire team.

Programmer Welfare

For the final principle, we'll take a look at programmer welfare and start with sustainable pace. By this, we mean that a developer should not work more than 40 hours in a week, and if they do have to do overtime one week, they shouldn't be expected to do overtime the following week. Extreme Programming projects utilize short iterations that make use of continuous integration, which means more value can be delivered to the business sooner than with more traditional waterfall development. Due to this fact XP projects produce more in at a more steady pace instead of having to have a mad rush at the end. A key enabler to achieve sustainable pace is to frequently merge code and always have an executable version of the product that is well tested with unit tests.

Well-tested, continuously integrated, frequently-deployed code and environments also minimize the frequency of unexpected production problems and outages and the associated after-hours, nights, and weekend work that is required.

Rules

The first version of the rules for Extreme Programming were published in 1999 by Don Wells. 29 rules are given in the categories of:

- Planning
- Managing
- Designing
- Coding
- Testing

Rules—Planning

The first category is planning. The first rule in this category is that user stories are written. User stories are used to document the use cases for the system being built. They are also used to create time estimates for the release planning meeting. User stories are used instead of large requirements documents, and they are written by the customers as requirements and functionality that the system needs to perform.

They are in the format of about three sentences of text written by the client in the customer's language. The user stories are not meant to be technical. User stories also help drive the creation of the acceptance tests. One or more automated acceptance tests should be created to verify the user story has been correctly implemented.

A planning meeting is used to create a release plan for the product. This plan is then used to break the release down into multiple iterations. It is essential in this meeting for technical people to make technical decisions, and business people to make business decisions. The idea of this release planning session is for the development team to estimate how long each user story will take to implement in ideal programming weeks. An ideal week is how long you imagine it would take to develop that story if you had absolutely nothing else to do and no distractions. The customer then prioritizes each story by their relative importance and value added to the system.

The development team should be aiming to release iterative and working version of the system to their customers often. Some development teams will deploy software into production every day. But more commonly, you'll want to deploy software into production every one or two weeks. At the end of every iteration, the development team should have tested, working, and production-ready software to demonstrate to customers. The customers will then decide whether to put that release into production. The iterative development adds agility to the development process. Divide your development schedule into a series of iterations of 1-3 weeks in length. You should keep the iteration length consistent, as this sets the pace for your product like a beating drum.

You shouldn't schedule programming tasks in advance. Instead, you use the iteration planning meetings at the start of each iteration to decide the priority for what will be done. Just-in-time planning is a more natural way to stay on top of changing user requirements.

Any failed acceptance tests from the previous iteration are also selected to be fixed in the next iteration. The customer chooses stories that have estimates that total out to the project velocity of the last iteration. The velocity is the average amount of work that can be completed in each iteration. The user stories and failed tests are broken down into the programming tasks that will support them. Programming tasks are written for each user story. While user stories are in the customer's language, tasks are in the developer's language.

Rules—Managing

Good communication is crucial for an Extreme Programming development team. You can make communication on your team more efficient by just removing any dividing barriers between desks to allow people to talk easier. The ideal working environment is an open-plan area where desks and computers are arranged to make pair programming easier. The team should either use shared computers or their computers are set up with a consistent development environment so that that code can be worked on any machine with minimal disruption. Try to include a large area for daily stand-up meetings, and add a conference table that gives the team a place to have more extensive group discussions.

To set your pace for a project, you need to take your iteration seriously. You want the most complete, tested, integrated, production-ready software you can get at each iteration. If your software is incomplete or riddled with defects, it is difficult to predict the amount of future effort required to release it. If you can not get your tasks completed within a set iteration, you can have another iteration planning meeting to re-scope the iteration to maximise your velocity.

Even if you are very close to the end of the current iteration, it is best to get the entire team refocused on a single completed task than many incomplete tasks. Working lots of overtime sucks the life out of your team. When your team becomes tired and starts lacking motivation, they will get less work done, not more. It is tough to make plans when your team does inconsistent amounts of work every month. Excessive overtime is very normally a result of bad planning and unrealistic goals. The purpose of your stand-up meeting is to get the whole team to communicate, so everyone knows what everyone else is doing.

A stand-up meeting every morning is used to communicate problems, solutions, and promote team focus. At a stand-up, everyone in the team should stand in a circle. By making the team stand you can avoid there being long conversations. It is more efficient to have one short meeting that everyone is required to attend than many meetings with few developers each. During a stand-up meeting, developers report at least three things. What was accomplished yesterday, what will be attempted today, and what problems are causing delays? The daily stand-up is probably one of the most valuable meetings your team can have to try and maintain momentum during an iteration as it encourages the team to bring issues out into the open so the team can fix them together.

The project velocity is a measurement of how much work is getting done on your project each sprint. To measure the project's velocity, you simply add up the estimates of the user stories that were finished during the iteration. You also total up the estimates of tasks completed during the iteration. Both of these measurements are used for the iteration planning. During the iteration planning meeting, your customers or project sponsors are allowed to choose the same number of user stories equal to the project's velocity measured in the previous iteration. Those user stories are split down into tasks, and the team is allowed to assign the same number of tasks equal to the previous iterations project velocity.

This method for working our velocity allows developers to recover and clean up after a challenging iteration and helps to average out estimates in the future. Your project velocity will go up by letting a developer ask the customer for another story when their work is finished early, and no clean-up tasks remain. You should try to move people around in the team to avoid serious knowledge loss and coding bottlenecks. If any one person on your team can work in a given area, and that person leaves or just has too much work to do, you'll find that your project progress reduces to a crawl.

Cross-training is a crucial thing to consider in companies trying to avoid developers becoming islands of knowledge in certain technical areas. This can be a particular problem if a developer who is regarded as an "expert" in one area decides to leave the organization. Moving developers around in the code base in conjunction with pair programming does your cross-training for you. Instead of having one developer who is an expert for a particular piece of the system, everyone on that team will gain knowledge about the system as a whole.

The Extreme Programming methodology isn't perfect, and it won't fit for all organizations and teams. You should follow the XP rules to start with, but do not hesitate to change what doesn't work out. This isn't a free license to do whatever you want though. The rules have to be followed until the team, together, decides to change them.

Rules—Design

It is always easier to complete a simpler design than a complex one. Therefore, you should always strive to make your designs simple. It's always faster, simpler and less expensive to replace more complex code early before you waste a lot more time on it. A system metaphor is a story that everyone, including your customers, programmers, and managers can tell about how the system works. It's a naming concept for classes and methods that should make it easier for a team member to guess the functionality of a particular class or method from its name only.

A system metaphor should be helpful in figuring out the overall design of the system. The metaphor should also help the team find a common vocabulary, and the metaphor is useful when helping everyone reach agreements about our requirements.

When developers are faced with a problem they don't know the answer to straight away, create spike solutions to figure out the answer. A spike solution is a simple prototype to explore potential solutions and options. Build a spike only to address the particular problem being investigated and ignore all other concerns. Most spikes are designed to be throwaway prototypes that never make it into production, so you don't need to labor over their design.

The goal is reducing the risk of a technical problem or increase the reliability of the user story's estimate. If this is a particularly tough problem, you can also put two developers on it to try and solve the problem. You should aim to keep the system uncluttered with extra code that you think may be useful later on. It is always tempting to add functionality now rather than later because we see exactly how to add it or because it would make the system so much better. We need to continually remind ourselves that we are not going actually to need it.

Rules—Coding

Code must be formatted to agree with your team's coding standards. It's these coding standards that keep the code consistent and easy for the entire team to read and refactor. Code that looks the same also helps to encourage collective code ownership. It used to be quite common for a team to have a coding standards document that defined how the code should look, including the team's best practices for styling and formatting. The problem with this is that people rarely read them, let alone follow them. Nowadays it's much more common to use a developer productivity tool to guide the user to using best practices automatically.

Popular tools in use today, certainly from a .NET perspective are ReSharper from JetBrains, CodeRush from Dev Express, and JustCode from Telerik. These are all paid for solutions though. If you want to use a FREE alternative, then you can look at StyleCop for the .NET platform. Visual Studio also has its versions of some of these tools built in, but it is quite common to supplement Visual Studio with an additional add-on.

Other development platforms will have their variants of these tools, either separate additions to their development environments or built-in to their IDEs. These tools are so unbelievably powerful that it makes it frictionless to write code that conforms to a set of coding standards

When you create a unit test first before writing out your code, you'll find it much easier and faster to create the code. The time it takes to create a unit test and then create the code to make it pass is about the same time as just coding it out in the first instance. Creating unit tests first helps the developer to consider what needs to be done and the system's requirements are firmly nailed down by the tests. There can be no misunderstanding the specification written in the form of executable code, and you'll also have immediate feedback during your work.

Under Extreme Programming, all code to be sent to production should be created by two people working together at a single computer. Pair programming will increase software quality without impacting the time to deliver. It can feel counter-intuitive at first, but two people working at a single computer will add as much functionality as two people working separately, except that it will be much higher in quality, and with increased code quality comes significant savings later in the project.

The best way to pair programming is just to sit side-by-side in front of the monitor and slide the keyboard backward and forwards between the two. Both programmers concentrate on the code being written.

Pair programming can sometimes be a difficult thing to sell to management as they just see two resources working on the same task at the double cost. They won't necessarily see that they are saving a lot of cost in the long run as the assumption is that code should be bug-free to start with.

Pair programming is a skill that takes time and effort to learn. Without force controlling the integration of code, developers test their code and integrate on their machines, believing all is well, but because of integration happening in parallel with other programming pairs, there can be combinations of source code which have not yet been tested together, which means integration problems can occur without detection. If ever there are problems and there is no clear-cut latest version of the entire source tree, this applies not only to the source code but to the unit test suite which must verify the source code's correctness.

If you cannot lay your hands on a complete, correct, and consistent test suite, you'll always be chasing bugs that may not exist and passing up on bugs that do. It is now standard practice to use some form of continuous integration system integrated with your source control repository. What this will do is when a developer checks in some code, the code is integrated with the main source code tree, built, and the tests are executed. If any part of this process fails, the development team will be notified immediately so that the issue can be resolved.

It's also common to have a source control system fail at check-in if the compile and test run fails. In <u>Team Foundation Server</u>, for example, this is called a gated build. Once you submit your code to the repository, the code is compiled on a build server, and the tests are executed. If this process fails for any reason, the developer would not be able to check-in their code. This process helps to ensure your code base is in a continual working state, and of high quality. Developers should be integrating and committing code into the source code repository at least every few hours or when they have written enough code to make their whole unit test pass. In any case, you should never hold onto changes for more than a day.

Continuous integration avoids diverging development, where developers are not communicating with each other about what can be reused or can be shared. Everyone on the team needs to work with the latest version of the source code, and changes to code should not be made to code that is out of date causing integration headaches. Each developer or pair of developers is responsible for integrating their code whenever a reasonable break presents itself.

A single machine dedicated to releases works well when the development team is co-located. This will be a build server that is controlled by checking commits from the source control repository like Team Foundation Server. This machine acts as a physical token to control release, and it also serves as an objective last word on what the common build contains. The latest combined unit test suite can be run before releasing when the code is integrated on the build machine, and because a single machine is used, the test suite is always up to date. If unit tests pass 100%, the changes are committed. If they fail for any reason, then the check-in is rejected, and the developers have to fix the problem.

Rules—Testing

Unit tests are one of the foundational cornerstones of Extreme Programming. First, you should decide on what unit testing framework you want to use. For .NET, for example, this might be NUnit or MSTest. Second, you should test all the classes in your system except trivial getters and setters, as those are usually omitted. You would also create your tests first before writing the actual application code. This doesn't mean you have to write all of the tests for the entire system up front, but before you tackle a new section, module or class, you would develop a set of tests as you go along with the coding.

While building up your tests and writing code to make the tests pass, you will, before you know it, have created a robust testing suite that can be executed over and over again. Unit tests are checked into the source code repository along with the code they test, and code without associated tests should not be released into production. If a unit test is found to missing, then it should be created at that time and checked in. Usually, the biggest resistance to dedicating this amount of time to unit tests is a fast-approaching deadline, but during the life of a project, automated tests can save you hundreds of times the cost it takes to create them by finding and guarding against bugs.

Another common misconception is that a unit test can be written in the last few months of a project. Unfortunately, without unit tests, the development drags on and eats up those last few months of the project and then some. Even if the time is available, an excellent unit test suite takes time to evolve. Just having a suite of unit tests is meaningless if any of the tests fail for any reason. If you find a test as failing, you should fix it straight away and not continue coding until all the tests are passing. It doesn't matter if it's your test or someone else's, but strive to get it fixed there and then.

If you have an automated continuous integration system setup, then you should be alerted straightaway if any of your tests start to fail. Even better, you'll be blocked from checking in the code if you have any check-in policies in force. When a bug is found, tests should be created to detect the bug and guard against it coming back. The debugging process also requires an acceptance test to be written to guard against it. Creating an acceptance test first before debugging helps customers concisely define the problem and communicate that problem to the programmers. Given a failed acceptance test, developers then start to create unit tests from a source-code-specific point of view.

Extreme Programming Diagram

Now that we have covered Extreme Programming in detail let's express some of what we have seen in an easy to understand diagram.

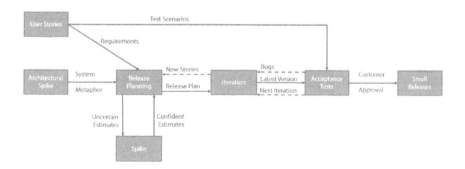

Figure 4 Extreme Programming (XP) Diagram

Here we have some of the different stages of XP, User Stories, Architectural Spikes, Release Planning, Development Spikes, Iterations, Acceptance Tests, and Small Releases. From the user story writing stage, we end up with a set of requirements and a series of test scenarios that form our acceptance tests.

From the architectural system spike, we end up with a system metaphor, which is a story that everyone, customers, programmers, and managers, can tell about how the system works. During the release planning phases, we determine what requirements are to be included in what releases, and when they should be released into. The developers and customers are both parts of this process.

If we are uncertain about particular estimates, we can create a spike application where a developer or developers spend a constrained amount of time to write a small example program to quickly solve the problem and therefore provide a more confident estimate.

The release plan then feeds into a development iteration where the code and unit tests are developed. Any new stories that come out during the iteration feedback into the release planning. From the iteration, you should have a working piece of software. This software should pass the acceptance tests set out from the user stories. If there are any bugs, then they are fixed by the developers.

There will typically be multiple iterations of a project. Once the acceptance tests pass from the iteration and the customer approves the system that has been developed in the iteration, a small release can take place at that point, which gives the users access to the real working code where they can start to reap the benefits early.

Scrum

In this chapter, we'll take a look at the Scrum methodology. Scrum is an iterative development framework where the value is delivered to the customer and users regularly. Scrum can be divided into three main areas:

- **Roles**—which contain the product owner, scrum master, and scrum team.
- **Ceremonies**—that contain the sprint planning, sprint review, and sprint retrospective ceremonies, and finally
- **Artefacts**—that contain product backlog, sprint backlog, and the release burn down chart.

First let's take a look at an overview of Scrum and its history.

Definition and History of Scrum

Scrum is an iterative and incremental agile software development framework for managing product development. It defines a flexible, holistic product development strategy where a development team works as a unit to reach a common goal. Scrum is a way to manage and organize a project, usually software development. In the Scrum world, instead of providing complete detailed descriptions that dictate how everything should be completed on a project, it is left up to the software development team to decide. This is because the team will know better how to solve the problem they are faced with.

Scrum encourages teams to be self-organizing and cross-functional where people are expected to be able to work in many areas and not just their personal niches. The Scrum team is self-organizing, in that there are no overall team leaders who decide which person will be doing which task and how the problem will be solved. Those are issues that are decided by the team as a whole.

Scrum was conceived by Ken Schwaber and Jeff Sutherland in the early 1990s. The term Scrum is borrowed heavily from the game of rugby to stress the importance of teams. Ken and Jeffs's paper showed that excellent performance in the development of new, complex products is achieved when teams, small self-organizing units of people, are given objectives instead of being handed tasks. Teams thrive when they are given objectives and a direction where they have room to make their own decisions on how to solve the objectives.

Teams require autonomy to achieve excellence. The Scrum framework for software development implements these principles described in this paper for developing and sustaining complex software projects. In February of 2001, Jeff and Ken were amongst 17 software development leaders who created a manifesto for agile software development.

Ken Schwaber, in 2002, founded the Scrum Alliance with Mike Cohn and Esther Derby, with Ken chairing the organization. In the following years, the highly successful certified scrum master programs were created and launched in 2006. Jeff Sutherland created his own company Scrum Inc, while still offering and teaching Scrum courses.

Ken left the Scrum Alliance in the fall of 2009 to found scrum.org to help improve the effectiveness of Scrum in the industry, mainly through their Scrum training. With the first publication of the Scrum Guide in 2010 and its incremental updates in 2011 and 2013, Jeff and Ken established a globally recognized body of knowledge of Scrum.

Overview of Scrum

Scrum is a project management framework that applies to any project with aggressive deadlines, complex requirements, and a degree of uniqueness. In Scrum, projects move forward by a series of iterations called sprints. Each sprint is typically 2-4 weeks in length. When describing the Scrum framework, it is easy to split it into three main areas. They are:

- **Roles**: which include the product owner, scrum master, and scrum team.

- **Ceremonies**: include the sprint planning meeting, sprint review, and sprint retrospective meetings

- **Scrum Artefacts**: and these include the product backlog, sprint backlog, and the burn down chart.

Let's first take a high-level look at these terms before we go into more detail. The product owner is a project's key stakeholder and represents the users for whom you are building the solution.

The product owner is a team member of the product management team or a key stakeholder or user of the system. It is quite common for a business analyst with domain experience to take on the product owner role for the development team who will regularly engage with the customers.

The scrum master is responsible for making sure the team is as productive as possible. The scrum master does this by helping teams use the scrum process by removing impediments to progress, by protecting the team from the outside, and so on. Their role is very much facilitating the team to steer their product to completion, and they act very much as a servant leader fulfilling the needs of the team. The typical scrum team has between five and nine people. A scrum project can easily scale into the hundreds. However, scrum can easily be used by 1-person teams, and often is.

This team does not include any of the normal software development roles such as developer, designer, architect, or tester. Everyone on the product works together as a team to complete a set of work they are collectively committed to complete within a sprint. Scrum teams tend to develop a deep form of camaraderie and a feeling that we're all in this together. At the start of a sprint, there is a sprint planning meeting that is held. During this meeting, the product owner presents the top items on the product backlog to the team. The scrum team then selects what they can complete during the coming sprint. That selected work is then moved from the product backlog to a sprint backlog, which is a list of tasks needed to complete the product backlog items the team has committed to finishing in the sprint.

At the end of each sprint, the team will demo the completed functionality from that sprints goal at the sprint review meeting, during which the team shows what they have accomplished during the sprint. Typically, this takes the form of demonstration of new features, but in an informal way. This meeting doesn't need to be very long or onerous to the development team but is a good forum to demonstrate the work completed in the sprint. Also at the end of each sprint, the team conducts a sprint retrospective, which is a meeting where the team, including the scrum master and product owner, will reflect on how well the Scrum process is working for them, and what changes they may wish to make for it to work even better.

Each day there is a meeting between the entire team called the stand-up. This meeting helps set the context for each day's work and helps the team stay on track. All team members have to attend the daily scrum. Ideally, everyone in the team stands in a circle. Everyone is made to stand so that their update is brief; otherwise, it can become uncomfortable. The team needs to answer three questions.

- What did I achieve yesterday?

- What do I plan to achieve today?

- Is there anything that is blocking me?

The product backlog is a prioritized list of features containing every desired feature or change in a product. There are multiple types of backlog in Scrum, the product backlog is a list of the desired features for the product, and a sprint backlog is a list of tasks to be completed within that sprint.

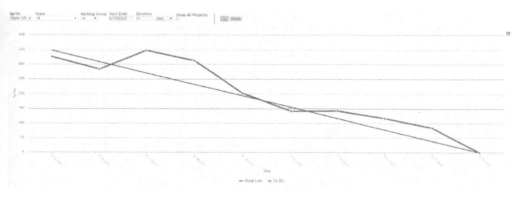

Figure 5 Example Burn down chart

On a Scrum project, the team will track its progress against a release plan on the burndown chart, as you can see in Figure 5. The burndown chart is updated at the end of each sprint by the scrum master. The horizontal axis of the chart shows the date and the vertical axis illustrates the amount of work remaining at the start of the sprint. Work remaining can be displayed in whatever unit the team prefers. This could be story points, ideal days or team days. Before we look at the Roles, Ceremonies, and Artefacts in more detail, let's look at a visual representation of the Scrum process.

Visualizing Scrum

The product backlog is a feature list that is prioritized and contains every desired feature or change to the product. When you have a sprint planning meeting, backlog items from the product backlog are selected to be implemented in the next sprint and placed into the sprint backlog. Once the sprint backlog has been identified from the product backlog, the team enters a 2-4 week sprint where they implement the items in the sprint backlog.

Product Backlog | Sprint Backlog | Daily Scrum Meeting | 2 – 4 Week Sprint | Potentially Shippable Product

Figure 6 The Scrum Development Process

Each day during the sprint, a brief meeting called a daily scrum is conducted. This meeting helps set the context for each day's work and helps the team stay on track. All the team members are required to attend the daily scrum. At the end of the sprint, the team should have a potentially shippable product that could go into production and give value to the end user. Now that we've had an overview of the scrum let's look at each of the roles, artifacts, and ceremonies in detail.

Scrum Roles

Scrum defines three main Roles:

- Product Owner

- Scrum Master

- Scrum Team

Usually, the Scrum team's product owner is the project's key stakeholder, but it could also be a business analyst who works closely with the business and the users of the system. Part of the product owner's responsibility is to have the vision of what he or she wishes to build and convey that vision to the rest of the scrum team. The product owner is key to successfully starting any agile software development project. The product owner works by maintaining the product backlog, which is a prioritized feature list for the product.

The product owner is usually a user of the system or someone from Marketing, Product Management, or anyone with an understanding of the users, the marketplace, the competition, and the future trends for the domain or type of system being developed. This could also be a business analyst who has an excellent grasp of the business domain. The product owner prioritizes the product backlog during the sprint planning meeting.

It is the development team that selects the amount of work that they feel they can complete each sprint and how many sprints it will take to complete their objectives. It is not the responsibility of the product owner to tell the development team how much work they should do in a sprint or how many sprints are required to complete the work. This should come from the rest of the development team who will be doing the actual estimates. Requirements are allowed to change within Scrum, and this change is encouraged, but these changes should come outside the sprint and ready for the next sprint planning meeting. Once a team starts on a sprint, it should remain focused entirely on delivering the work for that sprint.

The product owner's role requires a person with particular sets of skills, including availability to the team, business and domain expertise, and excellent communication skills. It is essential that the product owner is available to his or her team all the time, and that they should be committed to doing whatever is necessary to build the best product. Business and domain knowledge is important for agile product owners because he or she is the decision-maker regarding what features the product will have. That means a product owner should understand the market, the customer, and the business, to make the right decisions. Communication is a huge part of the product owner's role and responsibilities.

The product owner role requires working closely with the key stakeholders throughout the organization, so they must be able to communicate different messages to different people on the team about the product at any given time. The scrum master is responsible for making sure the Scrum team lives by the values and practices of Scrum.

The scrum masters' role is like that of a coach for the team, helping the team do the best work they possibly can. This involves removing any impediments or blockers to progress, facilitating meetings, and doing things like working with the product owner to make sure the product backlog is in good shape and ready for the next sprint. The scrum master role is commonly filled by a former project manager or a technical team leader, but it can be anyone.

People who are new to the scrum master role sometimes struggle with the apparent contradiction of the scrum master, who is both servant leader to the team and also someone with no authority as a team leader or manager. This contradiction disappears when we realize that although the scrum master has no power over scrum team members directly, the scrum master does have authority over the process.

The scrum master is there to help the team in its use of Scrum. They're a bit like a personal trainer who helps you stick with an exercise workout. A good personal trainer will motivate you, while at the same time making sure you don't cheat by skipping the hard exercise. A personal trainer cannot make you do any exercise you don't want to. Instead, the trainer reminds you of your goals and how you've chosen to meet them. To the extent that the trainer does have the authority that has been granted by the client, scrum masters are much the same. They have authority, but the authority is granted to them by the team.

The scrum master can say to the team, look, we're supposed to deliver potentially shippable software at the end of each sprint. We didn't do it this time. What we can do is make sure we do better on the next sprint. This is the scrum master exerting authority over the process. Something has gone wrong with the process if the team has failed to deliver something potentially shippable. But because the scrum master's authority does not extend beyond the process, the same scrum master should not say "because we failed to deliver some something potentially shippable last sprint, I want Kevin to review all the code before it gets checked in."

Having Kevin review the code might be a good idea, but the decision is not the scrum masters to make. With power limited to ensuring the team follows a process, the scrum master's role can be more challenging than that of a typical manager.

Project managers often have the fall-back position of "do it because I say so." The times when a scrum master can say that are limited and restricted to ensuring that scrum is being followed.

In a Scrum team environment, you don't have fixed roles and responsibilities, like front-end developer, back-end developer, database engineer, tester, etc. Everyone on the project works together to complete an agreed set of product objectives they've collectively committed to complete within the sprint. Because of this cross-discipline nature, scrum teams develop a sincere form of team spirit and feel like we're all in this together.

Scrum Ceremonies

In Scrum, there are four ceremonies that the scrum team will be involved with. These are the:

- Sprint planning meeting
- Sprint review meeting
- Sprint retrospective
- Daily scrum

The sprint planning meeting is attended by the scrum master, product owner, and the rest of the scrum team including developers, testers, architects and business analysts. Outside stakeholders and users may attend if they are invited along by the team, but generally, they won't be attending this meeting. During the sprint planning meeting, the product owner describes the highest priority features to the team. The team should then ask enough questions so they can turn a high-level user story of the product backlog into a more detailed set of tasks for the sprint backlog.

The product owner doesn't have to describe every item being tracked in the product backlog. A good rule of thumb is for the product owner to attend this meeting with enough work to talk about to fill up two sprints. This means that if the team is likely to finish what they thought they would get done in one sprint, the product owner is prepared with details of additional work and priorities.

By the end of each sprint, you are required to deliver a potentially shippable product. This means that at the end of each sprint the team has to produce a coded, tested, and usable piece of software. A sprint review meeting is held at the end of each sprint, and during this meeting, the scrum team shows what they have accomplished during the sprint as a live demo of the features. This meeting should be quite brief and not take up too much of everyone's time, as it'll also be attended by product customers and management whose time can be limited.

Participants in the sprint review typically include the product owner, the scrum team, the scrum master, management, customers, and developers from other products. During the sprint review, the product is assessed against the original sprint goal. Ideally, the team has completed each product backlog item brought into the sprint, but it's more important that they achieve the overall goal of the sprint. No matter how good a scrum team is, there is always the opportunity to improve.

Although a good team will always be looking for improvement opportunities, the team should set aside a brief dedicated period at the end of each sprint to reflect on how they are doing and find ways to improve. This takes place during the sprint retrospective meeting. The Retrospective is normally the last thing to be done in a sprint, and the whole team, including both the product owner and scrum master, should participate. A retrospective meeting should last for around an hour. However, occasionally a controversial topic will come up, or a team conflict will escalate, and a Retrospective could take longer.

During a retrospective meeting, the team should answer the following questions.

- What should we start doing?
- What should we stop doing?
- What should we continue doing?

The scrum master can run the sprint retrospective meeting by asking everyone just to shout out and contribute ideas. The scrum master can go around each person in the room asking them to identify anything to start, stop or continue. After an initial list of ideas has been thought through, teams will vote on specific items to focus on during the next sprint.

The daily scrum meeting is held every day, preferably in the morning. This meeting is crucial as it allows the team to understand where everyone else is within the sprint. Everyone stands in a circle during the meeting. By making everyone stand up, it ensures that their updates are brief, as standing up for too long is uncomfortable. The team has to answer three questions.

- What did you achieve yesterday?

- What will you achieve today?
- Is there anything blocking you?

If anything is blocking you, then you can work with the scrum master to resolve the blocking issue to enable you to continue.

Scrum Artifacts

As part of the Scrum process, there are three main artifacts you will use besides the actual delivered product. These are the:

- Product backlog
- Sprint backlog
- Burn down chart

In Scrum, the product backlog is a prioritized list of features containing short descriptions of all the desired functionality in the product. When using Scrum, it's not necessary to start a product with a long upfront effort to document all the requirements as you would in Waterfall. Typically a scrum team and its product owners will begin by writing down everything that they can think of for the backlog prioritization. This product backlog usually is always more than enough for the first sprint.

The scrum product backlog is then allowed to grow and change as more is learned about the product and its customers. A typical scrum backlog comprises the following different types of items:

- Features
- Bugs
- Technical work
- Knowledge acquisition

The main way for a scrum team to express features on the product backlog is by writing user stories. User stories are short, simple descriptions of the desired functionality told from the perspective of the user. An example would be, "as a pharmacist, I can dispense products from a customer's prescription, which then appear on the customers dispense items record."

There's also no difference between a bug and a new feature. Each describes something different that the user wants, so bugs are also put into the product backlog.

Technical implementation work and technical spike activities also belong in the backlog. An example of technical work would be, upgrade all developers' workstations to Windows 10, or migrate to using a continuous integration server for continuous delivery.

An example of technical spike work could be a backlog item about researching various JavaScript libraries and then making a technical decision. This may result in a small piece of work to solidify this knowledge. The product owner shows up at the sprint planning meeting with a prioritized product backlog and describes the top items to the team. The team will then determine which items they can realistically complete during the next sprint. The team then moves items from the product backlog to the sprint backlog. In doing this, they expand each product backlog item into one or more sprint backlog tasks so they can more effectively share work during the next sprint.

The sprint backlog is a list of tasks that are identified by the scrum master to be completed during the next sprint. During the planning meeting, the team works together to select some product backlog items to work on and identifies the tasks necessary to complete each story. Most teams also estimate how many hours each task will take for someone on the team to complete, although time-based estimates are almost always inaccurate. The reason for this is because each person will have different abilities and it will take them a different amount of time, based on experience, to complete the tasks. It is much better to estimate relative complexity and effort instead by using a Fibonacci number sequence or t-shirt sizes. A small t-shirt size might be equivalent to putting a field on the website and then persisting it to the database, and then everything else is estimated based on that relative complexity.

It's essential that the team selects the items and the size of the sprint backlog. Because other people are committing to completing the tasks, they must be the people to choose what they are committing to during the sprint.

The sprint backlog can be maintained as a spreadsheet, but it's also possible to use your bug tracking system or any number of software products designed specifically for Scrum or Agile. Team Foundation Server with the Scrum template, Jira, and VersionONE are common options to choose from.

Team members, during the sprint, are expected to update the sprint backlog as new information is available, but minimally once per day. Many teams will do this during the daily scrum. Once a day the estimated work remaining in the sprint is calculated and graphed by the scrum master, resulting in a sprint burndown chart.

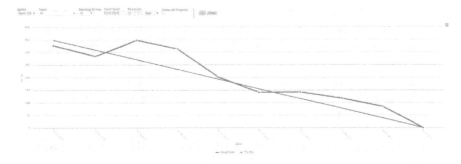

Figure 7 Example Burn down chart

The team will do as best as it can to move the right amount of work into a sprint, but sometimes too much or too little work is taken in during the planning. In this case, the team needs to add or move new tasks. On a Scrum project, the team tracks its progress against a release plan on a release burndown chart.

The release burndown chart is published at the end of each sprint by the scrum master. The horizontal axis of the burndown chart shows the sprints, and the vertical axis indicates the amount of work remaining at the start of each sprint. Work remaining can be shown in whatever unit the team prefers, story points, ideal days or team days.

The burndown chart is an essential part of any agile project, and it is a way for the team to see what is happening and how progress is being made during each sprint. One issue that may be noticed in the burndown chart is whether or not the actual work line is above or below the ideal work line, and this depends on how accurate the original estimates were. This means if your team keeps on overestimating their time required, the progress will always appear ahead of schedule. If they consistently underestimate the time required, they will always look on schedule.

Extreme Programming vs. Scrum

Now that we have taken a look at both Extreme Programming and Scrum let's take a look at some of the main differences between the two. Scrum teams work in iterations which are called sprints, and these sprints are generally between two and four weeks in length, although nothing is stopping you from having a one-week sprint if you have a small team.

Having such a short sprint can be problematic, though, if you have to fit in planning meetings, sprint reviews, and retrospectives all into one week. Extreme Programming teams work in iterations, and these iterations are 1-2 weeks in length. Once a sprint has started under Scrum, the scrum team doesn't allow any changes to that sprint until they are finished.

The team will continue as planned to the end of the sprint, and then do any pre-planning as necessary for the next sprint. With Extreme Programming, teams are much more amenable to change in their iteration. If a change is required, the team will hold another planning session and adjust their iteration accordingly. In Scrum, the product owner prioritizes the product backlog, but the team determines the sequence in which they will develop the backlog items.

The team is trusted and expected to set their own pace and workload within the sprint. The backlog will be prioritized, which causes work on the high-value items first, but the team picks the order for these high-value items to be implemented.

In Extreme Programming, the teams work in a strict priority order as set out in the planning sessions, and tend not to deviate from that order. Scrum does not prescribe any engineering practices for the developers, as it is more of a lightweight project management framework. Extreme Programming, on the other hand, is a very engineering-based methodology that defines many engineering practices like test-driven development, pair programming, and continuous integration.

Extreme Programming comes with many rules that can be hard for new teams to adopt. In my experience, what tends to happen is teams adopt scrum, as it is a lightweight framework for managing your agile project, and then introduces different engineering practices from Extreme Programming as deemed necessary. For example, at the time of writing this book, I am working on a scrum team where we do test-drive development and continuous integration and delivery.

Closing Summary

In this book, we first looked at the more traditional Waterfall and V-Model development methodologies and discussed how they don't work very well for modern large-scale projects due to the big bang nature of deployments.

We then looked at the agile development philosophy and how it focuses on delivering value to the customer in smaller increments.

Agile covers four main guiding values, and these values are what the different agile software development practices are based on.

These values are:

- Individuals and interactions over processes and tools
- Working software over comprehensive documentation
- Customer collaboration over contract negotiation
- Responding to change over following a plan

Next, we took a detailed look at the Extreme Programming development methodology.

Extreme Programming is an engineering based discipline that contains many rules that need to be followed. Extreme Programming is a useful framework but teams can be put off by its initial complexity to follow all the rules and can be difficult to follow for a team that is trying to transition into agile from the waterfall.

Scrum, on the other hand, is a more lightweight project management framework that doesn't contain any engineering practices. What is quite common is for a team to adopt scrum due to its more lightweight nature and then pick various engineering disciples from extreme programming that suit the team like Test Driven Development and Continuous integration.

If you enjoyed this book, then you might also like my other book called A Gentle Introduction to Lean Software Development, available on Amazon as a Kindle e-book or paperback.

Made in the USA
Coppell, TX
26 October 2022

85289407R00049